Shojo Beat

Yona of the Dawn

36

Story & Art by

Mizuho Kusanagi

Yona of the Dawn

Volume 36

CONTENTS

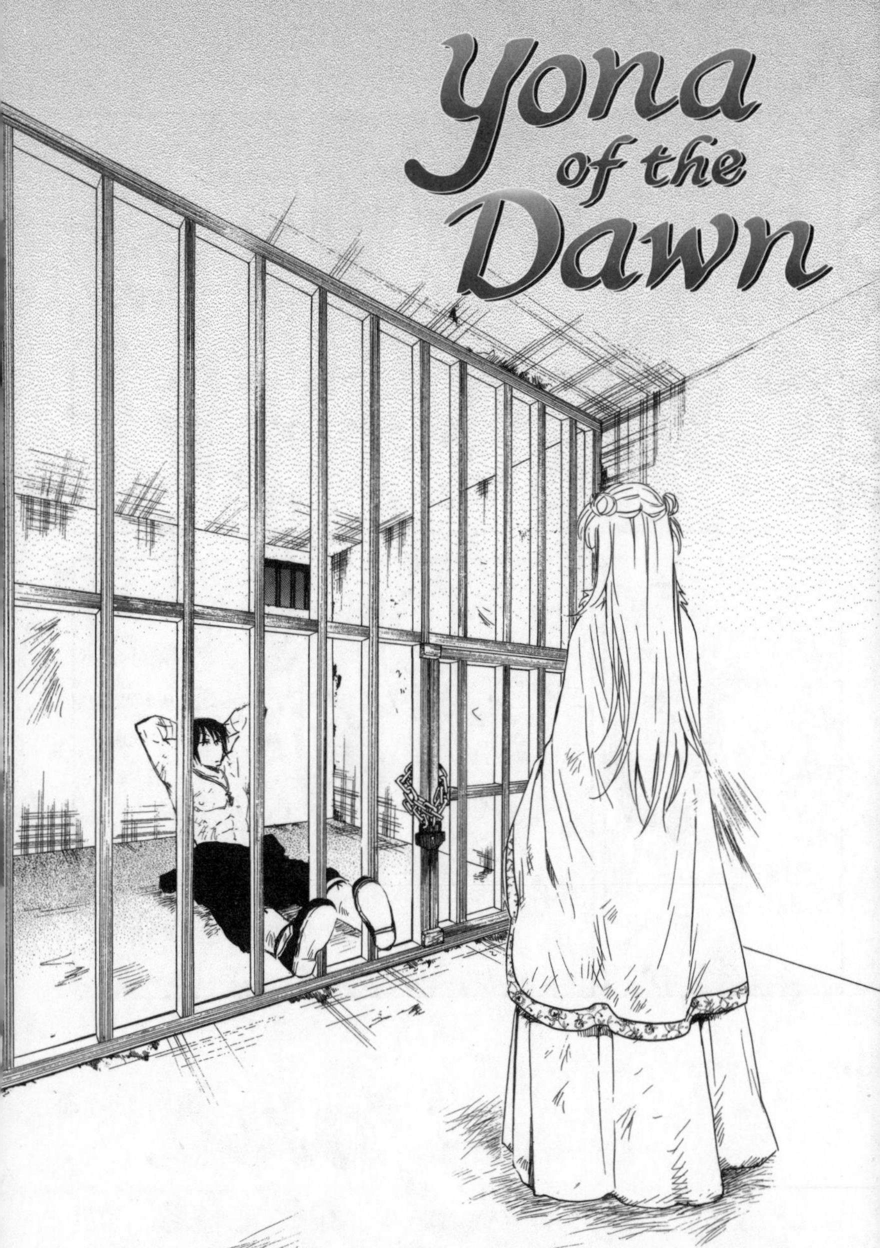

CHAPTER 205: A CRY IN THE NIGHT

Yona of the Dawn

WASN'T THERE A GUARD OUT THERE?
WAS THERE?
YOU DON'T STRIKE ME AS SOME RESCUING PRINCE.
...
The Princess
LOOK AT THOSE MUSCLES. WHAT DID HE DO TO GET THROWN IN HERE?
HE COULD BE USEFUL...
DO YOU *WANT* ME TO BE A PRINCE WHO SAVES YOU?

OH.
NAH.
I'M FINE.
...
R-really ...?
You won't run away with me?
TEARFUL
WHY'D YOUR SPEECH CHANGE LIKE THAT, PRINCE?
WHO'RE YOU SUP-POSED TO BE?
I ACCIDEN-TALLY SPOKE NORMALLY TO BEGIN WITH.
So much for seducing him.
DON'T YOU WANT OUT OF THERE?

I'M FINE FOR NOW.
FOR NOW?
THERE WERE FOUR GUARDS OUT THERE! AREN'T YOU SOME RUTHLESS CRIMINAL?
THEY'RE CLEARLY GOING TO KILL YOU.
FOUR? WHAT A JOKE. THEY'RE REALLY NOT EXPECTING ME TO BREAK OUT, HUH?
IF SU-WON DECIDES TO KILL SOMEONE, THAT'S THAT.
EVEN A RELATIVE OR A WOMAN.
ARE YOU RELATED TO SU-WON?
Oh!
OF COURSE NOT.

DO YOU KNOW WHERE THE PALACE GARDEN IS?
SURE.
I'VE BEEN THERE MANY TIMES...
WHAT ABOUT IT?
I'LL HELP YOU OUT.
HUH?

I SAID I'M FINE.
I DON'T EVEN KNOW WHO YOU ARE.
FIND SOMEONE ELSE.
I'VE CHOSEN YOU.
HOW COME?

YOU'RE EASY TO TALK TO.
UH, THANKS?
FELLOW PRISONERS SHOULD GET ALONG—
THROB
...
Prison doesn't usually build friendships.
SLUMP
WHAT'S WRONG?
HEY...
NNH...

THROB
DAM-MIT...
AM I DOOMED TO DIE WHEREVER I GO?
THROB
CLANK
CLANK
COME ON.
CREAK...
LISTEN ...

DO AS I SAY.
COME WITH ME.
LEAD ME TO THE GARDEN AND I'LL LET YOU GO.
I REFUSE.
...
ISN'T THERE ...
...SOMEONE OUT THERE YOU WANT TO SEE?

THERE IS.
DESPERATELY, ACTUALLY.
BUT RIGHT NOW, IF I OBEY MY EMOTIONS, SHE'LL TRY TO PROTECT ME.
I DECIDED TO WAIT HERE...
...AND NOT CAUSE HER TROUBLE.

YOU'RE FREE TO GO IF YOU WANT.
BUT EVEN WITH THAT DOOR OPEN, I'M STAYING PUT.
THROB
SWAY...
SLAM

Huff...
Huff...
Huff...
UGH...
WHICH WAY'S THE GAR-DEN?
RUSTLE
RUSTLE
HOH...
Hoh!

HOH, COME ON OUT...
HOH ...!
LET'S GO HOME ...

THROB
LET'S GO HOME ...

I CAME HERE PLANNING TO LEAVE EVERYTHING BUT HOH BEHIND.
I DON'T KNOW WHERE TO GO NOW.
RUSTLE
Ah!

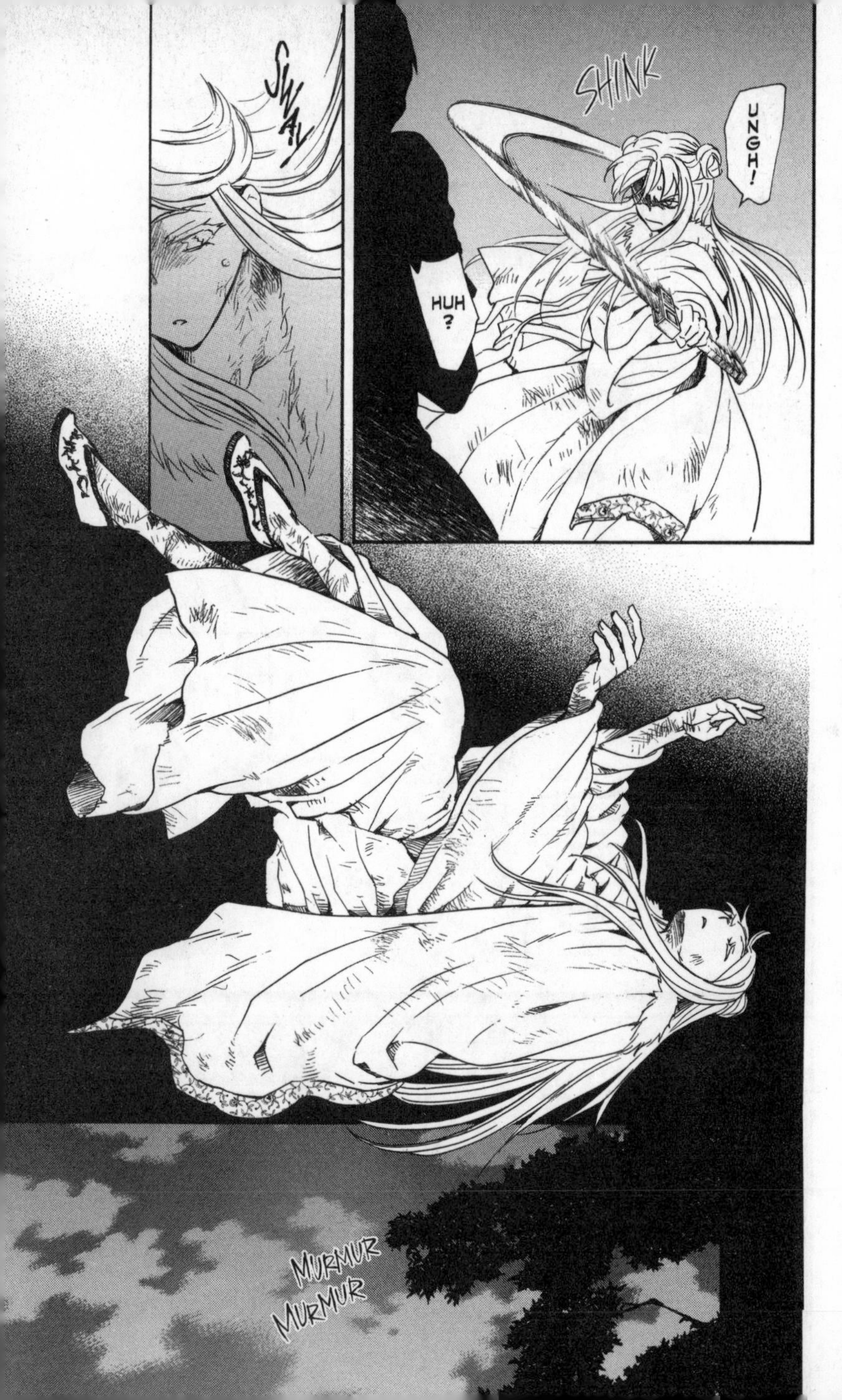

SHINK
UNGH!
HUH?
SWAY
MURMUR MURMUR

Hoh...
SHE'S SCARED...
IT'LL BE OKAY. I'LL TAKE YOU TO MEINYAN TODAY.
Hang in there.
YOUR HIGHNESS!
APPARENTLY MEINYAN ISN'T IN HER CELL.
WHAT?!
DID SHE ESCAPE?
LIKELY SO.
BUT STRANGELY...

...THE FOUR GUARDS AT LORD HAK'S CELL WERE FOUND STABBED.
WHAT'S MORE, HIS CELL WAS UNLOCKED FOR SOME REASON.
?!
WE SUSPECT IT'S CONNECTED TO MEINYAN'S ESCAPE, SO LORD HAK IS BEING QUESTIONED.
HAK WAS IN HIS CELL, RIGHT?
THAT'S RIGHT. I'M TOLD HE WAS IN THERE WORKING OUT.
Working out...
WE'RE CURRENTLY SEARCHING FOR MEINYAN.

IT'LL BE OKAY. I'M SURE THEY'LL FIND HER SOON.

BUT IF THEY DO FIND HER...
...HER SITUATION WILL BE EVEN WORSE BECAUSE SHE ESCAPED.

WHERE COULD SHE BE RIGHT NOW?
I FIND IT STRANGE THAT HAK'S GUARDS WERE STABBED AND HIS CELL WAS UNLOCKED...

HAK DIDN'T DO ANY OF THAT.
OF COURSE NOT.

BUT I CAN'T HELP THINKING THAT SOME-THING UNTOWARD HAPPENED.
DON'T GO DOWN THAT PATH.
Not in front of the young lady.
UNTO-WARD?
OH, COME TO THINK OF IT...

...THERE ARE RUMORS THAT MEINYAN SEDUCED HER GUARDS...

I KNEW IT! SHE WAS TRYING TO GO AFTER HAK!

THWACK

YOU'RE DEFINITELY MISTAKEN!

AH, YUN.

SO DILIGENT! STILL STUDYING HERBS?
UH-HUH.
THE SOUTH KAI DELEGATES LEFT, BUT IF WE GO TO WAR, I'D LIKE YOU ON THE MEDICAL TEAM.
I'LL... THINK ABOUT IT.

IF THE DELEGATION LEFT, I GUESS YONA'S NO LONGER SUSPECTED OF MURDER.
THANK GOODNESS THEY DIDN'T TAKE HER AWAY...

I DON'T KNOW IF OUR ALLIANCE WITH KING SU-WON IS GOING WELL...
...BUT...
...THE PEOPLE IN HIRYUU PALACE DON'T SEEM SO BAD WHEN YOU TALK TO THEM.
I THINK IT WAS GOOD FOR ME TO COME HERE.

IT'S A BIT EMBARRASSING THAT I USED TO THINK I KNEW EVERYTHING ABOUT THEM...
...BASED ONLY ON MY BAD EXPERIENCES WITH THEM.
BUT I STILL DON'T THINK IT'S RIGHT FOR THEM TO SAY THAT WHAT HAPPENED TO YONA COULDN'T BE HELPED.
FWMP
Let's see...
OH!
YOU'RE AWAKE?

IT'S BEST IF YOU DON'T GET UP.
...

I'LL CHANGE OUT YOUR BANDAGES.

WHO ARE YOU?!
SWING
AGH!
I DON'T HAVE MY SWORD.
I COULD TAKE THIS KID BAREHANDED...
...
SWAY...
DON'T MOVE TOO MUCH. YOUR WOUNDS WILL REOPEN.
I'M YUN. AN APOTHECARY.
AN... APOTHECARY...?

WHERE ...
WE'RE INSIDE HIRYUU PALACE.
YOU PASSED OUT FROM YOUR INJURIES YESTERDAY.
IT SEEMED RISKY TO LEAVE YOU, SO I BROUGHT YOU HERE.
I DON'T WANT TROUBLE. JUST STAY AND RECOVER QUIETLY, OKAY?
IS THIS A TRAP?
HE HAS TO BE SUSPICIOUS OF ME...
SOME DUMPLING SOUP?
It's good for stimulating an empty stomach.
CAUTIOUS

This is incredible.
I'M GLAD YOU'RE EATING.

THERE'S MORE IF YOU WANT.

sip...

KLAT
KLAT

WE'RE FINALLY HEADING BACK TO YUUKYOU.
KLAT
KLAT
THAT WAS A MISERABLE EXPERI- ENCE.

Ha ha ha!
EVEN IF HIS IMPERIAL HIGHNESS ORDERS IT, I'D LIKE A BREAK FROM DIPLOMATIC MISSIONS FOR A WHILE.
HMM? SOME- ONE'S COMING.
CLOP
CLOP
IT'S GENERAL VAL.

I'VE COME TO ESCORT YOU.

MUCH APPRECI- ATED, GENERAL.

WE'RE EXHAUSTED. THERE WERE MANY ISSUES BESIDES RANTAN'S DEATH.

KOHKA'S KING AND THAT PRINCESS ARE DEVIOUS.

...

MAY I ASK WHERE LADY MEINYAN IS?
LADY MEI-NYAN?
WE WERE TOLD SHE'D RETURNED TO YUUKYOU AHEAD OF US.
I DARESAY SHE'S FAWNING OVER HIS IMPERIAL HIGHNESS BY NOW.
WHAT A WONDERFULLY WILD PRINCESS SHE IS.
CHAPTER 205 / THE END

HAVING LEFT KOHKA, THE DELEGATION FINALLY REACHED YUUKYOU IN SOUTH KAI.

CHAPTER 206: DISCARDING THINGS ONE BY ONE

EM-
PEROR
CHAGOL.

THE
DELEGA-
TION HAS
RETURNED.

DID YOU BRING THAT PRINCESS YONA WHO KILLED RANTAN?

Yona of the Dawn

HUH?
DID SU-WON APOLOGIZE? OR BEG FORGIVENESS?
W-WE'RE TERRIBLY SORRY.
KING SU-WON PREVENTED US FROM PURSUING ANYTHING CONCERNING RANTAN...
WHAT DID YOU GAIN FROM THIS TRIP?
CHAGOL SUPREME RULER OF SOUTH KAI
ANYTHING ASIDE FROM ELIMINATING THAT MEDDLESOME RANTAN?
YOU SHOULD HAVE REFUSED THE FUNERAL AND RETURNED AT ONCE, FOOLS.
NOW TELL ME...
WHERE IS MEINYAN?

UNFORTUNATELY, LADY MEINYAN'S CURRENT WHEREABOUTS ARE UNKNOWN.

WE'RE SO SORRY! IN KOHKA, WE WERE TOLD SHE HAD DEPARTED AHEAD OF US. WE HAD NO IDEA...

I-I'M SURPRISED SHE'S NOT BACK YET...

EMPRESS SHANTE
FIRST CONSORT

KNOWING HER, SHE'S ENJOYING HERSELF SOMEWHERE.

...

SHE'S ALWAYS SO... UNINHIBITED.
TH-THAT'S RIGHT! WHEN LADY MEINYAN MET KING SU-WON, SHE WAS EXTREMELY FRIENDLY WITH HIM.

SHE LATER SEEMED STRANGELY CONFIDENT THAT HE'D WANT TO SEE HER AGAIN.
SOON AFTERWARD, SHE WAS GONE.
MY! ARE YOU SUGGESTING SHE FOUND HER WAY INTO HIS BED?
I WONDER IF THAT'S WHY SHE JOINED THE DELEGATION...

VAL.
GENERAL HITTAN.

IS IT TRUE THAT MEINYAN— ER, LADY MEINYAN— HAS GONE MISSING?

I'M NOT CERTAIN, BUT SHE HASN'T RETURNED.

I HAD A FUNNY FEELING ABOUT THAT CONFERENCE FROM THE START.

YOU MEAN LORD RANTAN'S DEATH?
HE WAS CLEARLY ELIMINATED BY ONE OF US.
DO YOU THINK LADY MEINYAN GOT MIXED UP IN THAT?

NO... I'M SURE SHE KNEW IT WOULD HAPPEN.
BEFORE LEAVING, SHE CAME TO SAY GOODBYE.
HOW are YOU? ♡ I'LL BE aCCOMPaNYING THE DeLeGaTION.
Ho ho ho ho!
HUH?
I CAME BECAUSE HOH SAID SHE WANTED TO SEE YOUR FACE.
SEE YA.
I FELT LIKE SHE MIGHT NOT BE PLANNING TO COME BACK.
SHE'D BEEN WANTING TO GO TO HIRYUU PALACE.
EVEN A FAVORED CONCUBINE MUST HAVE ENEMIES.
SHE WAS BEST SUITED TO BEING A GENERAL THOUGH.

WHAT CAN SHE HAVE HOPED TO DO...
...IN A NATION WE MIGHT CRUSH?
I'M BEING RE-LEASED?

WE'RE REQUESTING YOUR CO-OPERATION.

WE NEED YOU TO TRACK DOWN AND CAPTURE THE ESCAPED WOMAN KNOWN AS MEINYAN.

YOU WANT *ME* TO CAPTURE HER?
SHE'S FROM SOUTH KAI AND HAS TOP SECRET INFORMATION CONCERNING KOHKA.

SHE ALSO KILLED SEVERAL SOLDIERS. WE MUST CAPTURE HER BEFORE THERE ARE MORE CASUALTIES.

IS THE INFORMATION ABOUT SU-WON?

...

TELL ME. YOU LOCKED ME UP TO PROTECT THAT SECRET.

IF YOU'RE DESPERATE ENOUGH TO LET ME OUT, THIS MUST BE HUGE.

KLAK

...

KLAK KLAK

WELL...
I'M GOING OUT FOR A BIT.

MAKE SURE YOU REST.
SHUT
CREAK
SHUNK
FOUND IT.
Who stands a sword up in a cup-board?
CREEAK
Oh!

I HEARD THE ESCAPED WOMAN'S A LONG-HAIRED BEAUTY. I'D LIKE TO GET A LOOK!

TH-THMP

ARE YOU STUPID? SHE KILLED SEVERAL GUARDS.

STAY ALERT.

TH-THMP

THEY'RE SEARCHING FOR ME.
I NEED TO FIND HOH AS SOON AS POSSIBLE.
THAT YUN KID HAS TO BE SUSPICIOUS OF ME.
HE MIGHT BRING SOMEONE...

"I HEARD THE ESCAPED WOMAN'S A LONG-HAIRED BEAUTY."
IT'S GETTING LATE.
TAK
I need to hurry back.
TAK

WHAT ARE YOU DOING?

JOLT

LOOKING FOR SOMETHING.

I SEE ...

WHY'D YOU CUT YOUR HAIR?

DASH

FWMP
NNH ...
OH, COME ON.
WHAT ARE YOU DOING? YOU'RE STILL INJURED.
HOH ...
"HOH"?
SHE LOOKS LIKE THIS...
About this big
DOES SHE MEAN PU-KYU?
SHE MUST BE HUNGRY...
...
WIPE
WIPE

I'LL LOOK FOR HOH TOMORROW WHEN THERE'S MORE LIGHT. FOR NOW...

...LET'S HEAD BACK AND HAVE SOME STEAMED BARLEY.

I DON'T HAVE A BATH, BUT I'LL HEAT SOME WATER SO YOU CAN WASH UP.

WITH JUST THE TWO OF US THERE? ARE WE GOING TO WASH EACH OTHER?

You're a naughty kid, aren't you?

OF COURSE NOT!

I've got a partition.

splish

UGH, I'M FEELING AWKWARD SINCE SHE SAID THAT.
I'M FINE WITH MEDICAL EXAMS THOUGH.
GRIND GRIND
Are we bathing each other?
I'LL PASS!

Heh!

AN INJURED WOMAN WITH HER HAIR HACKED SHORT...
FOR SOME REASON...

...IT'S MAKING ME THINK OF...
...WHEN I FIRST MET YONA.

NOK NOK

YES? WHO IS IT?

At this hour?

HEY.

HUH?
WHAT?!
HOW ARE YOU HERE ALL OF A SUDDEN?
UH... I WONDERED HOW YOU WERE.

I'VE BEEN WORRIED SICK ABOUT YOU! I FEEL LIKE I HAVE AN IDIOT SON WHO LEFT THE COUNTRYSIDE TO BECOME A FOOT SOLDIER.

YUN, I'M AIMING TO BE A PERSONAL BODYGUARD.

Certainly not a foot soldier.

WHAT'S UP? ARE YOU ON LEAVE?

YEAH... DO YOU HAVE A MINUTE?

HUH? UM, RIGHT NOW'S A BIT... CAN WE TALK OUTSIDE?

YOU HAVE COMPANY?

NOT EXACTLY, BUT...

HUH? GENERAL JU-DO?

KLAK

WHY ARE YOU—

I'M GOING IN.

HUH?

HOLD ON...

TOPPLE
LUNGE

WHA —?!
SLA
SH

KLANG
KLANG
GRAB
KRASH
AGH!

SWING
AAH!
THUD
NNH ...

Huff
Huff
YOU'RE ...
...THAT MAN WHO WAS DOING SIT-UPS IN THE DUNGEON... WEREN'T YOU STAYING IN YOUR CELL?
I WAS ASKED TO CAPTURE YOU.
HUH? DUNGEON? CAPTURE HER?
LONG STORY. SHE WAS WITH THE SOUTH KAI DELEGATION. SHE'S ALREADY KILLED SEVERAL SOLDIERS.

I HEARD SHE WAS WANDERING THE PALACE WITH A SWORD, SO I CAME TO CHECK ON YOU.
I had no idea she'd be here.
SHE CAN'T BE ALLOWED TO LIVE.
WE'RE TAKING HER IN.
WHAT?
THROB
OF COURSE.
YOU'RE AN ENEMY TOO.
THROB
THROB
I FIG-URED...
I'M NOT GOING TO LET THEM KILL ME.
I WON'T BE KILLED...
CHAK

...BY THE LIKES OF SU-WON!
DASH
WAIT, THUNDER BEAST!
THUNDER BEAST?!
THIS GUY?!

THIS IS DANGEROUS, YUN. STEP ASIDE.

I-I'M SORRY.

BUT ...

...SHE'S... INJURED.

SHE'S KILLED OUR SOLDIERS.

SHE DESERVES NO PITY.

YOU'RE RIGHT ...

BUT STILL ...

STILL ...

I DID THINK SHE SEEMED DANGEROUS...

...BUT...
... SHE'S ...
...MY PATIENT.

IT MAY NOT BE RIGHT TO DEFEND SOMEONE WHO'S KILLED OTHERS...
...BUT I DOUBT SHE WANTED TO DIE EITHER.
I DISLIKE VIO-LENCE.
I'M ACTING SELFISHLY, AND THAT MIGHT CAUSE A LOT OF PEOPLE TROUBLE.
I DON'T KNOW WHAT THE RIGHT THING IS.
I'M SORRY. BUT...
...I'M HERE TO STUDY MEDICINE.

I CAME HERE BECAUSE I WANT TO HEAL PEOPLE.

THAT MEANS EVERY-THING TO ME.

CHAPTER 206 / THE END

CHAPTER 207:
THIS SIDE

Jaeha

Yona of the Dawn

SLUMP
...
Ah!
ARE YOU OKAY?
DID YOUR WOUNDS REOPEN?
N-NO...
THAT'S NOT WHAT'S HURTING.
IT'S THE CRIMSON SICK-NESS...
CRIMSON SICK-NESS?
YOU CAN'T HEAL ME OF IT.
ONE WAY OR THE OTHER ...
...I'LL BE DEAD SOON.

I DOUBT SU-WON'S LONG FOR THIS WORLD EITHER.
GETTING RID OF ME WON'T CHANGE THAT.
SU-WON DOESN'T HAVE LONG...?
WHAT DO YOU MEAN? I'VE NEVER EVEN HEARD OF THIS ILLNESS...
YUN.

RATTLE
SOME-
ONE'S
OUT-
SIDE...!
TAK
SLAM

MIN-SU!

IT'S JUST YOU...
S-SORRY FOR STARTLING YOU.
I felt like my heart was about to stop.

I HEARD LORD HAK WAS HEADED HERE AFTER BEING RELEASED.
But...
WE'LL TALK LATER, GENERAL JU-DO.

DASH

SHE'S SUFFERING FROM SOME DISEASE I DON'T KNOW.
...

I'LL GIVE HER THIS MEDICINE.
LET'S GET HER LAID DOWN.

MIN-SU!
GEN-ERAL JU-DO.

I SPOKE WITH ADVISOR KEISHUK EARLIER.
I'LL BE LOOKING AFTER HER.

WHAT ?!
UNDER SURVEIL-LANCE, OBVI-OUSLY.

SHE CAN HELP US LEARN MORE ABOUT THIS ILLNESS.
IT'S FOR HIS MAJ-ESTY'S SAKE.
WAIT.
WE SHOULDN'T LET THAT BOY HEAR ABOUT THIS.
MEINYAN'S ALREADY TOLD HIM. IT'S TOO LATE FOR THAT.
IF YOU TRY TO IMPRISON OR INJURE YUN LIKE YOU DID WITH ME, YOU'LL BE GOING THROUGH ME.
THERE IS ONE WAY...
...TO PROTECT YUN.

THAT'S FOR HIM TO BECOME MY ASSISTANT.

YOUR ASSIS-TANT?!

IF YOU DO THAT, YOU WON'T BE HARMED.

It's a sneaky move though.

WHAT ...

...DO I HAVE TO DO?

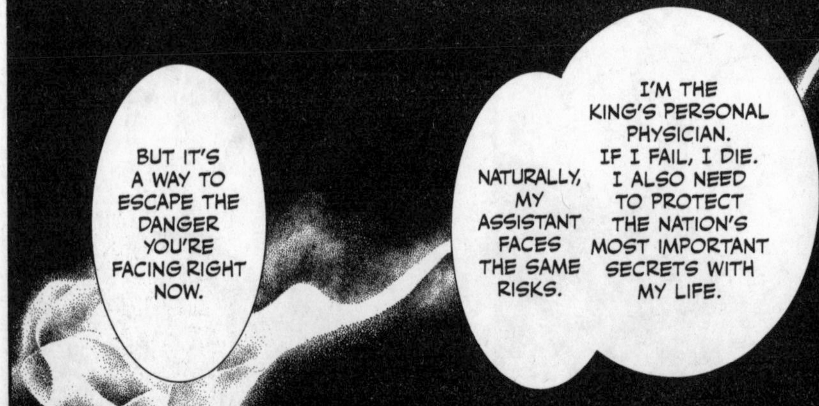

I'M THE KING'S PERSONAL PHYSICIAN. IF I FAIL, I DIE. I ALSO NEED TO PROTECT THE NATION'S MOST IMPORTANT SECRETS WITH MY LIFE.
NATURALLY, MY ASSISTANT FACES THE SAME RISKS.
BUT IT'S A WAY TO ESCAPE THE DANGER YOU'RE FACING RIGHT NOW.

I ALREADY WANTED TO ASK FOR YOUR HELP, BUT I DIDN'T WANT TO GET YOU INVOLVED IN THE ROYAL FAMILY'S SECRETS.

BUT I OVERHEARD WHAT YOU SAID JUST NOW.

WHEN IT COMES TO MEDICINE, I'M CONFIDENT THAT YOU'D NEVER BETRAY A PATIENT.

SWP

I'LL REASON WITH HIS MAJESTY AND ADVISOR KEISHUK.

YUN, WILL YOU JOIN ME AS THE KING'S...

... PERSONAL PHYSICIAN?

I'LL STILL BE ABLE TO TREAT HER TOO, RIGHT?
ALL RIGHT.
I'LL DO IT.

VERY WELL.
LET'S KEEP MEINYAN IMPRISONED IN THE PALACE.

YOUR MAJESTY... WOULD YOU GRANT MY NEW ASSISTANT YUN PERMISSION TO LEAVE THE PALACE?
PERMIS-SION TO LEAVE?

I'D LIKE HIM TO HARVEST SOME HERBS I HAVEN'T TESTED YET.

...
I REALIZE THAT THE CRIMSON SICKNESS IS NO ORDINARY ILLNESS.

BUT AS YOUR PHYSICIAN, I'D LIKE TO EXPLORE ALL POSSIBLE OPTIONS.

VERY WELL.
ONE MORE THING.
MAY LORD HAK ACCOMPANY YUN AS HIS GUARD?
ISN'T THERE ANYONE ELSE WHO CAN GO?
THE PLANT IS INCREDIBLY RARE, AND IF SOMEONE FROM THE PALACE GOES, THEY MIGHT NOT BE ALLOWED TO HAVE ANY.
AND AS WITH THE SEARCH FOR MEINYAN, IT'D BE BEST IF IT'S DONE BY SOMEONE WHO ALREADY KNOWS THAT YOU'RE ILL.
I DOUBT HAK WOULD FETCH MEDICINE FOR ME.
ACTU-ALLY...

...HE'S ALREADY AGREED.
ADVISOR KEISHUK, I DIDN'T THINK YOU'D ALLOW...
...LORD HAK TO LEAVE.
HE PROBABLY WON'T CAUSE PROBLEMS FOR HIS MAJESTY WHILE PRINCESS YONA AND THE DRAGON WARRIORS ARE IN THE PALACE.
I WOULDN'T NORMALLY TAKE SUCH A DANGEROUS RISK...

...BUT RIGHT NOW, OUR HIGHEST PRIORITY MUST BE HEALING HIS MAJESTY.

AS IT STANDS, I CAN ONLY WAIT FOR HIM TO RECOVER.

IT MAKES ME WANT TO PRAY TO SOME HIGHER POWER...

MIN-SU SAYS HE'LL CARE FOR YOU WHILE I'M GONE.
That sleep medicine was really effective.

YOU SHOULD PROBABLY KNOW THAT SHE'S CHAGOL OF SOUTH KAI'S FAVORITE CONCUBINE.
?!

TH-THAT'S WHO SHE IS?!
I HAD NO IDEA SHE WAS SO SKILLED WITH SWORDS...
SHE'S CERTAINLY NOT SOME ORDINARY PRINCESS.
SHE'S THE MOST GIFTED SWORDS-WOMAN I'VE EVER SEEN.

THUNDER BEAST, IF YONA HEARS THAT, SHE'LL WANT TO START TRAINING IMMEDIATELY.
HER HIGHNESS IS AMAZING FOR HAVING LEARNED SO MUCH SO QUICKLY.
I HEARD YOU'RE THE THUNDER BEAST.
YIKES! You startled me.
YOU WERE AWAKE?
I HEARD "THUNDER BEAST."
THAT'S ME. SO?
DO YOU BELONG TO PRINCESS YONA?
Well...
I GUESS SO.

I SAID I'D TAKE EVERYTHING OF HERS FOR MYSELF...
HOW DO YOU EXPECT TO DO THAT...?
IT'S NOT FAIR.
SHE HAS THE DRAGON WAR-RIORS, ...
...THE THUNDER BEAST, A HEALTHY BODY, A COMFORT-ABLE LIFE...
I DOUBT ANYTHING I SAY WOULD GET THROUGH TO YOU...
...BUT I HOPE YOU'LL LISTEN TO THE PERSON WHO'S DESPERATELY TRYING TO CURE YOUR CONDITION.
NO, IT'S FINE.
I DON'T...
...MIND.

I'LL BE AWAY FOR A BIT.

I'LL MAKE SURE YOU GET BETTER.

WAIT AND SEE.

THERE'S NO WAY...

...I'LL GET BETTER.

BUT...

...EVEN IF I DIE...

...I'LL ALWAYS THINK OF YOU AS THE PERSON WHO SAVED MY LIFE.

HEY, THUNDER BEAST?

HM?

I'M GLAD YOU'RE COMING, BUT...

TMP TMP

ARE YOU OKAY BEING AWAY FROM YONA?

WHITE SNAKE AND THE OTHERS ARE THERE. SHE'LL BE OKAY.

THAT'S TRUE, BUT...
...YOU WEREN'T AIMING TO BE *MY* BODYGUARD, RIGHT?
HA HA!
SOMETIMES I WISH I COULD SPLIT INTO THREE PEOPLE.

ALL THREE OF YOU WOULD JUST RUN TO YONA.
I'D SAY THAT TOO, BUT IT SOUNDS OBNOXIOUS.

ANYWAY, THE FIRST ONE...
...WOULD MAKE SURE...
...YOU'RE PRO-TECTED.

THE SECOND WOULD KEEP WHITE SNAKE AND THE OTHERS ALIVE.
AND THE THIRD WOULD KEEP HER HIGHNESS FROM CRYING.
THAT'S A LOT.
I SURE AM BUSY, HUH?
LET'S GET GOING AND HURRY BACK.
PLEASE WAIT, YOUR HIGH-NESS!

?!
FWISH

YONA ...!
LEAP
FWUMP

JUST IN TIME!
Couldn't quite catch her
...HEY.

YONA ...
Um...
Are you injured?
YUN, IT'S BEEN AGES!

MIN-SU FILLED ME IN.
YOU'RE HIS ASSISTANT NOW, AND YOU'RE OFF TO GET SOME SENJU HERBS, RIGHT?
Y-YEAH.
YONA, YOU SHOULD'VE SAID YOU WANTED TO COME DOWN.
OH. SORRY.
TMP

I WAS IN A RUSH. I COULDN'T HELP MYSELF.

COULDN'T HELP YOURSELF?!

THAT WAS DANGER-OUS!
DON'T COPY DROOPY-EYES!
You'll break some-thing.
IT'S FINE. I'VE DONE IT PLENTY OF TIMES BEFORE.
DON'T DO IT AT ALL!

DROOPY-EYES, KEEP A CLOSE EYE ON HER. THERE'S NO TELLING WHAT SHE'LL GET UP TO OTHERWISE.
Too true.
IT'S REALLY OKAY! I'VE BEEN TRAINING.
YONA, IF YOU RILE UP THE THUNDER BEAST TOO MUCH, HE'LL SPLIT INTO THREE TO KEEP TABS ON YOU.

THERE'S NO NEED FOR THAT. ALL THREE OF YOU SHOULD STAY WITH YUN.

SHE DOESN'T NEED EVEN ONE OF ME?

PLEASE TAKE CARE OF YUN...

YUN IS TAKING ON A DANGEROUS JOB WHILE KEEPING A LIFE-THREATENING SECRET.
I UNDER-STAND... ...MY MIS-TRESS.
SHA
HONESTLY...
I NEVER GET A CHANCE TO TELL HER...
...I MISSED HER OR...
HAK...

DON'T LOWER YOUR HEAD.

I CAN'T TELL HIM I WANT TO SEE HIS FACE...

TELL CAPTAIN GI-GAN I SAID HELLO.
OKAY.
Hoh...

HUH? YOU HAVE A FRIEND, PU-KYU?

Hoh...

...
HOH?

HOH!

YOU'RE HOH, AREN'T YOU?!

Hoh...

"HOH"?

I FOUND HOH!

Huh?

What?

CHAPTER 207 / THE END

CHAPTER 208: AFRAID OF NEVER WAKING UP

Yona of the Dawn

PRINCESS YONA?!
PRIN-CESS YONA?
DON'T WORRY.
I'LL BE ONLY A MINUTE.
LEAP
HOH!
HUH?

HOH—
Pu-kyu!
YOU'RE NOT HER!
!
Hoh...
HOH!
THERE'S ANOTHER CUTIE?!
AND YOU'RE FRIENDS?!
Ao is a cutie...
HOH...
THANK GOODNESS.
SHE SEEMS WELL.
SHE WAS LOST. AO BROUGHT HER TO US.

I'M GLAD YOU'RE REUNITED.
YUN WAS SO HAPPY WHEN HE SAW HER.
PRINCESS YONA...
...TOOK CARE OF HOH?
OKAY, WE'RE OFF.
Come on, Ao.
WAIT!
UM...
COULD I TOUCH HER?
HUH?
YOU MEAN AO?
YES. HER.

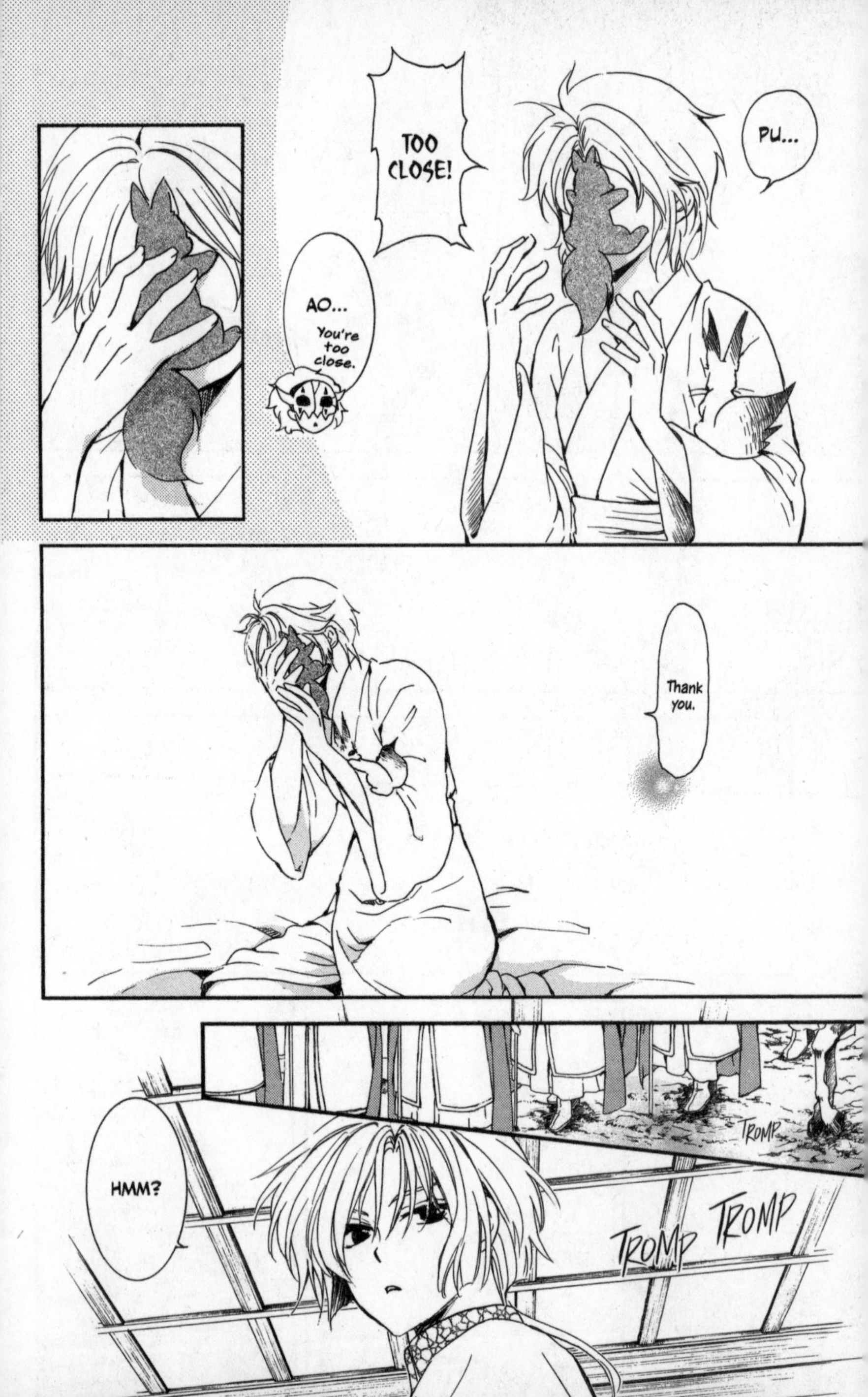
PU...
TOO CLOSE!
AO...
You're too close.
Thank you.
TROMP
TROMP TROMP
HMM?

TROMP

TROMP

WHAT'S THAT NOISE?

IT SEEMS THE FIRE AND WATER TRIBE TROOPS HAVE ARRIVED.

TROMP

TROMP

AL-READY?

TROMP

WE'RE ON THE BRINK OF WAR.

TROMP

TROMP

TROMP

KOHKA'S ENTIRE ARMY WILL ADVANCE TOWARD SOUTH KAI SOON.

I THOUGHT YOU'D AT LEAST WAIT FOR HAK TO RETURN.
ISN'T HE GOING INTO BATTLE TOO?
THE ENEMY WON'T WAIT FOR US.
BUT THAT'S FINE.
EVEN WITHOUT THE THUNDER BEAST, OUR FORCES ARE STRONG ENOUGH THAT WE SHOULD BE VICTORIOUS WITHOUT MAJOR LOSSES.
DON'T UNDER-ESTIMATE THEM...
...OLD MAN.

"OLD MAN" ...?
SOUTH KAI HAS TWICE AS MANY SOLDIERS AS KOHKA AND CAN REQUEST REINFORCEMENTS FROM NORTH KAI IF NEED BE.
EMPEROR CHAGOL'S GAINED A LOT OF POWER THESE PAST FEW YEARS.
HE'LL DO ANYTHING TO WIN.
EVEN IF KOHKA HAS BEEN DOING WELL RECENTLY...
...SU-WON IS AFFLICTED WITH THE CRIMSON SICKNESS. HIS TROOPS HAVE NO FUTURE.

SOUTH KAI HAS SOME TREMENDOUS GENERALS TOO.
ARE YOU... REALLY CHAGOL'S FAVORITE CONCUBINE? ARE FOUL-MOUTHED WOMEN BELOVED IN SOUTH KAI?
OH, THAT.
I WAS RAISED IN A MALE HOUSEHOLD AND I USED TO BE A GENERAL.
DAINTY SPEECH WON'T RALLY THE TROOPS.
This is how I usually speak.
A GENERAL?!

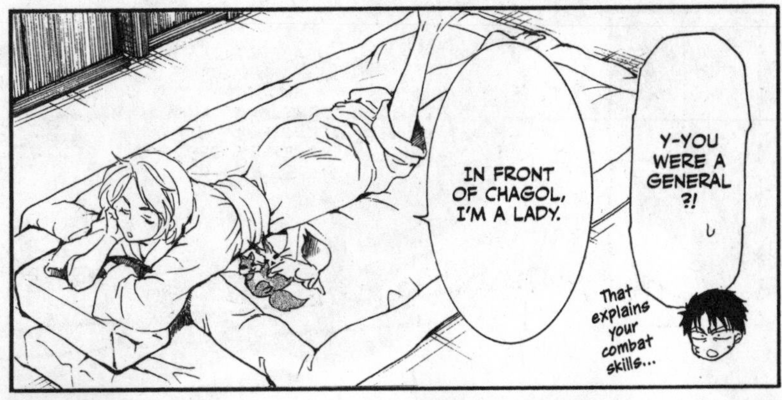
Y-YOU WERE A GENERAL?!
That explains your combat skills...
IN FRONT OF CHAGOL, I'M A LADY.

REMEMBER HOW CHARMINGLY I TRIED TO SEDUCE YOU.
YOU CALL THAT CHARMING? RIDICULOUS.

What? She tried to seduce you?
DON'T LOOK AT ME.

YOU WENT FROM GENERAL TO FAVORED CONCUBINE ...?

IF I GAIN POWER AND STATUS BY GETTING CLOSE TO CHAGOL...

...I MIGHT BE ABLE TO GO TO HIRYUU PALACE ONE DAY.
MAYBE I'LL MEET THE FOUR DRAGON WARRIORS.
I'D BE ABLE TO SHARE MY PAIN WITH SU-WON, WHO SHARES MY BLOODLINE.
ALL THE BLOOD I COUGHED UP TO GET HERE WAS FOR NOTHING.
KOHKA WILL FAIL.
IT STANDS NO CHANCE AGAINST KAI.
KOHKA HAS THE FOUR DRAGONS.
HOW MANY SOLDIERS KAI HAS IS IRRELEVANT!

I'M RELIEVED THAT HAK WENT WITH YUN.
TROMP
TROMP
BUT NOW I FEEL A BIT UNEASY.
TROMP
TROMP
IT'LL BE FINE. THEY'LL BE BACK SOON ENOUGH.
TROMP
TROMP
TROMP
KNOCK
KNOCK
YELLOW DRAGON ZENO.
HIS MAJESTY WISHES TO SEE YOU.

ONLY ZENO?
YES.
IT WON'T TAKE LONG.
I'VE BROUGHT HIM.

THANKS.
PLEASE COME IN.
...
THANK YOU FOR COMING.
IF YOU'RE GOING TO TAKE A BREAK, YOU SHOULD GET SOME REAL REST.

UNFORTU-NATELY, I'M TOO SHORT ON TIME.
PLEASE SIT WHEREVER YOU LIKE.
WHAT DO YOU WANT?
Well...
I'M BUSY, SO I'LL GET RIGHT TO THE POINT.
ZENO, ARE YOU AT ALL INTERESTED IN THE THRONE?

NOT AT ALL.
WHAT ABOUT POLI-TICS?
NOT AT ALL.
AS I EX-PECTED.
HUH? IS THAT ALL YOU WANTED TO ASK?
I FIGURED I HAD NOTHING TO LOSE.
AND IF I'D BEEN INTEREST-ED?
YOU'D NEED TO BE TRAINED TO RULE, SO I HAD TO KNOW AS SOON AS POSSIBLE.

IS THAT HOW YOU SAW ME?
I CONSIDERED YOU A POSSIBILITY AND THOUGHT I'D TAKE A CHANCE.
IS THERE NO ONE ELSE WHO CAN SUCCEED YOU?
THE SKY TRIBE HAS MILITARY OFFICERS AND CIVIL SERVANTS WHO'VE BEEN EDUCATED SINCE CHILDHOOD.
THEY'RE SKILLED, BUT THEY LACK A DECISIVE FACTOR.
I'D HOPED FOR SOMEONE WITH A BROADER VISION, UNCON-STRAINED BY THEIR TRIBE...
...WITH STRONG VITALITY AND SELF-DISCIPLINE.
THEN I REAL-IZED...
...AN EXCEPTIONAL INDIVIDUAL WHO CAN'T BE KILLED HAD APPEARED BEFORE ME.

SOMEONE WHO KNOWS HISTORY WELL, WITHOUT BIASES.
NO GOOD COULD COME OF AN IMMORTAL TAKING THE THRONE.
YOU'D BE FINE. YOU'VE LIVED 2,000 YEARS AND YOUR SPIRIT HASN'T BEEN CRUSHED.
IT HAS BEEN.
COUNT-LESS TIMES.
IN THAT CASE, I'M SURE THOSE AROUND YOU WOULD HANDLE THINGS.
SCARY ...
BUT IF YOU'RE NOT INTERESTED, THAT'S HOW IT IS.
WE'RE DONE TALKING.
AND THE YOUNG LADY...?

ISN'T THE YOUNG LADY A POSSIBILITY?
I'VE NEVER CONSIDERED THAT.
...
OH— THERE'S ONE MORE THING I WANTED TO ASK.
YOU KNEW ABOUT MY MOTHER, RIGHT?
WE WEREN'T REALLY ACQUAINTED, BUT I'VE KEPT AN EYE ON THE CRIMSON DRAGON KING'S DESCENDANTS OVER THE CENTURIES.

HOW MANY OF THOSE DESCENDANTS HAVE RECOVERED FROM THE CRIMSON SICKNESS?
...
NONE.
I FEEL BAD FOR THE LAD AND THE FELLOW. THE SICKNESS ISN'T SOME-THING SENJU HERBS CAN CURE.
WHY DIDN'T YOU TELL THEM THAT?
THE LAD AND YOUR PHYSICIAN STILL WOULD HAVE NEEDED TO TEST IT FOR THEMSELVES!

YOUR ILLNESS REMINDS ME OF THE OTHER DRAGONS.
THEY'RE FATED TO HAVE SHORT LIVES.
YOU'RE SAYING THE OTHER THREE DON'T HAVE LONG TO LIVE?
IT'S THE COST OF UNEARTHLY POWERS AND BLOOD.
THAT COST WILL BE DEMANDED BY THE NEXT DRAGON, WHETHER THEY WANT IT OR NOT.

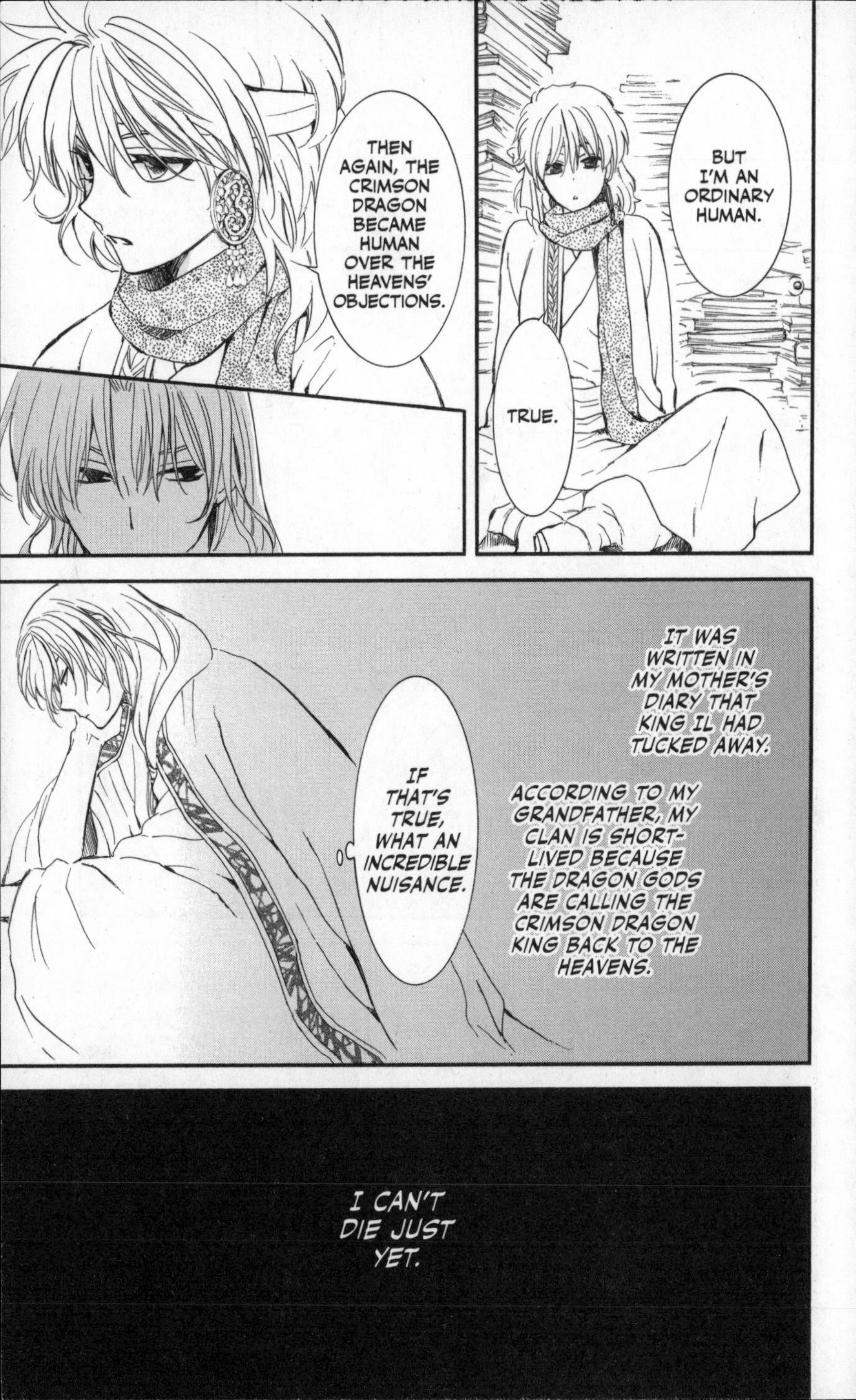

BUT I'M AN ORDINARY HUMAN.

TRUE.

THEN AGAIN, THE CRIMSON DRAGON BECAME HUMAN OVER THE HEAVENS' OBJECTIONS.

IT WAS WRITTEN IN MY MOTHER'S DIARY THAT KING IL HAD TUCKED AWAY.

ACCORDING TO MY GRANDFATHER, MY CLAN IS SHORT-LIVED BECAUSE THE DRAGON GODS ARE CALLING THE CRIMSON DRAGON KING BACK TO THE HEAVENS.

IF THAT'S TRUE, WHAT AN INCREDIBLE NUISANCE.

I CAN'T DIE JUST YET.

NOT UNTIL I DEFEAT THE KAI EMPIRE AND MAKE KOHKA INTO A POWERFUL NATION THAT CAN'T BE THREATENED.
UNTIL IT REACHES THAT IDEAL STATE...
...I ABSOLUTELY CANNOT...
ARE YOU SLEEPY?
I TOOK SOME MEDICINE EARLIER.
I CAN'T SPARE THE TIME TO SLEEP, BUT...
...THE PAIN INTERFERES WITH MY WORK...
LACK OF SLEEP WILL SHORTEN YOUR LIFE.
...
I DON'T HAVE ...
... ENOUGH TIME ...

NNN...
EVEN WITH ALL THE TIME YOU COULD WANT...
...NOTHING WILL EVER GO JUST AS YOU WISH.
BUT SOMEDAY... MY JOURNEY WILL COME TO AN END.
AND WHEN IT DOES...

...I'LL TRY TO GRANT YOUR WISH.
EVEN IF IT MEANS TURNING MY BACK ON THE GODS.
CHAPTER 208 / THE END

SOUTH KAI,
YUUKYOU.
THE PHOENIX
PALACE.

CHAPTER 209:
A SECRET ORDER

Yona of the Dawn

YES... I HAD THAT GREAT HONOR.
LADY MEINYAN WAS STILL A GENERAL THEN.
WERE YOU INTIMATE?

NO!
NOTHING OF THE SORT.

WELL, WHAT-EVER.
THAT CAT'S STILL WANDERING KOHKA AND HASN'T COME BACK TO ME.
COULD YOU GO AND BRING HER HOME?

YOU...WANT ME TO GO TO HIRYUU PALACE...?
NOT AS A MESSENGER.
I WANT YOU TO STEAL HER BACK.
CRUSH
STEAL HER? WE DON'T KNOW WHAT HER CURRENT CIRCUMSTANCES IN HIRYUU PALACE ARE—
I DON'T CARE.
MAYBE SHE'S THEIR KING'S MISTRESS NOW.
MAYBE SHE'S ALREADY DEAD.

...
BUT NO MATTER WHAT'S BECOME OF HER, WE MUST GO AFTER THIS RUNAWAY CAT.
BUT... WAR IS LOOMING.
AS A GENERAL, I LEAD THOUSANDS OF MEN—
ANOTHER GENERAL WILL COVER FOR YOU.
MAKE NO MISTAKE, YOU ARE ONE OF THE BEST OF SOUTH KAI'S EIGHT GREAT GENERALS.
THAT'S WHY I'M ENTRUSTING MY STRAY CAT TO YOU.
WAFT...

SHIVER

I'LL GRANT YOU THE USE OF THE DROMOS.

USE THEM WELL.

THE DROMOS—EMPEROR CHAGOL'S PERSONAL ASSASSINATION SQUAD!

TO USE *THEM* MEANS...

WAIT—WHAT ARE YOU SENDING ME TO DO?

YOU'LL INFILTRATE HIRYUU PALACE ONCE THE BATTLE BEGINS, WHEN IT'S LIGHTLY GUARDED.

SINCE YOU'RE GOING ALL THE WAY THERE, I WANT YOU TO...
...CARVE OUR EMPIRE'S MARK ONTO KUUTO.

KLAK

...
Sigh...
WHAT A PAIN ...

I'D FAR RATHER BE AT THE FRONT.

PARDON ME, GENERAL VAL!

WE HEAR THERE'S ABOUT TO BE A BIG BATTLE WITH KOHKA.
ALLOW ME TO WISH YOU THE BEST OF LUCK.
THIS IS A GOOD LUCK CHARM.
THANKS.
giddy giddy
...
"WELL, AREN'T YOU POPULAR?"
"WHY NOT MARRY ALL OF THEM?"

TWO YEARS AGO ...
GENERAL VAL!
GENERAL, WELL DONE ON YOUR MILITARY EXERCISES. ♡
ALLOW ME TO GET YOU SOME REFRESH-MENTS.
ME TOO! ♡
ME THREE! ♡
WELL, AREN'T YOU POPULAR?
WHY NOT MARRY ALL OF THEM?
EEEE! GENERAL MEINYAN! ♡

GENERAL, YOU HAVE SUCH SLENDER ARMS! HOW CAN YOU HOLD YOUR OWN AGAINST MEN?

HEH HEH...

SHE FIGHTS DIRTY.

SHE EVEN POISONS HER WEAPONS.

SHUT UP.

And today, she's kind of smelly.
What?!
THEY SURE ARE CLOSE, HUH?
YEAH.
I'm jealous.

I'M WEARING PERFUME TODAY.
It's impossible for me to be smelly.
Hey, you're wearing a lot of makeup too.
HOW COME?
TODAY I HAVE AN AUDIENCE WITH EMPEROR CHAGOL.

OH?

HIS IMPERIAL HIGHNESS HAS SHOWN INTEREST IN BEAUTIFUL FEMALE GENERALS.

IF ALL GOES WELL, I COULD BECOME A CONCUBINE.

Oho ho!

Heh...

DON'T SCOFF.

Want me to break your nose?

ARE YOU OKAY WITH IT? WE MIGHT NOT BE ABLE TO BE SO FRIENDLY ANYMORE.

ARE YOU SURE YOU DON'T WANT TO CONFESS YOUR LOVE WHILE YOU STILL HAVE A CHANCE?

I'd reject you though.

NO NEED. I'M FINE.

SOON AFTERWARD, IT ACTUALLY HAPPENED.

WHETHER IT WAS BECAUSE SHE ADMIRED THE EMPEROR OR BECAUSE SHE WANTED STATUS...
...I THOUGHT IT WAS FINE AS LONG AS SHE WAS HAPPY.
BUT THEN...
COULD YOU...
...LOOK AFTER HOH FOR A BIT?
I'M SURE SHE'LL BE SAFE WITH YOU.
...SURE. I DON'T MIND...
Hoh...
BE PATIENT, HOH. I'LL BE BACK.
HEY...
SHE BEGGED ME NOT TO ASK ANY QUESTIONS AND LEFT.
WHAT'S WITH THOSE INJU-RIES?
SHE USED TO GET PLENTY BATTERED AS A GENERAL, BUT...
Hoh...

I NO LONGER HAD ANY WAY OF KNOWING...
...WHAT WAS HAPPENING IN THE PALACE.
I'M GOING TO BRING HER BACK...
BUT WHAT'LL HAPPEN TO HER...
...ONCE SHE'S HERE?

KLAT
KLAT
KIN PROVINCE, EARTH TRIBE TERRITORY
LORD GEUN-TAE!

YEAH?
HOW ARE THINGS GOING?
JUST LOOK! WE HAVE SO MUCH IRON ORE.
UNTIL RECENTLY, WE ALWAYS RAN SHORT THANKS TO SOUTH KAI'S PILLAGING.
BUT THANKS TO THE GUARDS YOU STATIONED HERE, WE CAN FOCUS ON OUR MINING WITHOUT WORRY.
GLAD TO HEAR IT.
HOLD OUT JUST A BIT LONGER!

VERY SOON NOW, KING SU-WON AND AN ARMY OF WARRIORS FROM ALL OF KOHKA'S TRIBES WILL DEAL WITH SOUTH KAI.

ALL OF THE TRIBES?!

INCREDIBLE!

UNTIL THEN, THE EARTH TRIBE ARMY WILL DEFEND YOU!
IF ANYTHING HAPPENS, LET ME KNOW.
W-WE WILL!

I'M SO GRATEFUL FOR LORD GEUN-TAE.
HIS SON WAS JUST BORN, SO HE MUST WANT TO GO BACK TO CHISHIN PALACE AS SOON AS POSSIBLE.

YET HERE HE IS, PERSONALLY GUARDING THE BORDER.
HIS MERE PRESENCE MAKES THE VILLAGE FEEL MORE VIBRANT.

!
LORD GEUN-TAE!
IT'S SOUTH KAI!
ARE THEY HERE TO RANSACK US AGAIN?
YAAH!
HOW MANY?
A HUN-DRED.
GRAB
RIGHT, THEN.
THIS IS A PRELIMINARY SKIRMISH.

LORD GEUN-TAE IS HEADING INTO BATTLE!
FOLLOW ME...
EARTH TRIBE WAR-RIORS!
YAAH!
CLOP CLOP CLOP
CLOP
CLOP
CLOP CLOP CLOP

CLOP
CLOP CLOP
CLOP
CLOP
CLOP
GAAAH!

AAGH!
CLOP
CLOP
CLOP
CLOP
A TRUE GOD OF BATTLE!
I NEVER IMAGINED GETTING TO SEE LORD GEUN-TAE FIGHT UP CLOSE...!
H-HE'S TOUGH.
Urk...
HOW ARE WE STRUG-GLING AGAINST SO FEW?

SCATTER THEM!
YAAAH!
CLOP CLOP CLOP
CLOP CLOP CLOP

FWOOO
HURRAH!!
LORD GEUN-TAE!
LORD GEUN-TAE!
WOW!

HEY! COME BACK, KALGAN!
SCAMPER
LORD GEUN-TAE!

THAT'S INCREDIBLE! YOU PRETTY MUCH BEAT THEM SINGLE-HANDEDLY!
YOU WERE JUST LIKE HAK!

HAK?
YEAH! HAK STRIKES DOWN HIS ENEMIES LIKE LIGHTNING WITH HIS GLAIVE.

THERE'S ONLY ONE PERSON THAT CAN BE.
HEY, LEMME TOUCH YOUR SWORD!
KAL-GAN!
NOT NOW. LATER ON—
GET DOWN, BOY!
SWIP
THOK
THOK

SEEP
SLUMP
LORD GEUN-TAE!

NGH ...
...
LORD GEUN-TAE!
EEEK!
THIS IS TER-RIBLE!
CARE-FUL!
THERE ARE STILL SOLDIERS AROUND!

FWIP FWIP
AAGH!
FWIP
DON'T PANIC.
RE-SUME BATTLE FORMA-TION!
BUT —!
NEVER MIND ME!
GO!
LORD GEUN-TAE...
LORD GEUN-TAE!
AAGH!
...
Guh...
FWIP

LORD GEUN-TAE!
SH

SLA

CLATTER
CHAPTER 209 / THE END

A special thanks to these people who always help me out!

My assistants who've worked with me → Mikorun, C.F., Ryo Sakura, Ryo, and my little sister...

My editors → Hasegawa (Sho), my previous editors, and the *Hana to Yume* editorial office...

Everyone who is involved with the sale of *Yona*, the printing house, and Naato...

Everyone involved in the production of *Yona*-related goods...

My family and friends, who always encourage and support me...

My longtime readers and those who've only recently started reading...

I'm really thankful for all the help I receive from everyone who is involved in my work. I'm sorry for causing you so many problems. And I'm very thankful to my readers who continue to follow me.

Thanks to all of you, *Yona of the Dawn* has reached volume 36!

CHAPTER 210:
A GRAVE INJURY

Yona of the Dawn

HAK!
KALGAN, YOUOKAY?
I'M FINE, BUT LORD GEUN-TAE...
HE PRO-TECTED ME...
YUN! HELP GEUN-TAE!
O-OKAY.
KALGAN, IT'S DANGER-OUS. KEEP BACK.

FWIP
FWIP
AAGH!
CURSES! WE CAN'T GET NEAR THEM.
OUR ARROWS CAN'T REACH THEM EITHER.
IS LORD GEUN-TAE ALL RIGHT?!
I DON'T KNOW!
CALM DOWN!
STAY TOGETHER!

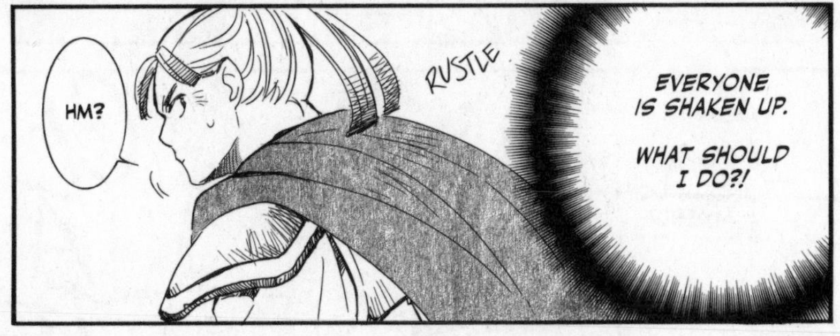

EVERYONE IS SHAKEN UP.
WHAT SHOULD I DO?!
RUSTLE
HM?

CLACK
CLACK
WHO ARE YOU? WHAT ARE YOU DOING?!
SORRY, I'M JUST BORROWING YOUR BOW FOR A BIT.
ARE YOU A VILLAGER?! YOU NEED TO STAY BACK.
WAIT— I'VE SEEN HIM BEFORE.
HUH? AREN'T YOU FROM THE WIND TRIBE? THE THUNDER BEA—
CLATTER
LET ME INTRODUCE MYSELF.

KRI!
I'M A NEW RECRUIT...
!
...IN THE SKY TRIBE ARMY.

THOK
GUH!
THOK
GAH!
HE *HIT* THEM?!
FWIP
FWIP
NNH
THOK THOK

MURMUR
THEY ALL HIT HOME ...!
THAT SKY TRIBE ROOKIE IS AMAZING.
NO, THAT'S THE THUNDER—
FWIP
THAT GUY!
GET THAT MAN!
KRII
UGH ... HERE THEY COME!
...
LET ME RIDE BEHIND YOU.
HUH?!

SH
CLOP CLOP CLOP
VEER RIGHT!
O-OKAY!
DODGE
FWIP
FWIP

SMASH
!
TUG
!
ER...
FIRE!
FWP
NOW LEFT!
FWP
EEP!
WIP

SNATCH

HOLD MY GLAIVE.

SHOVE SHOVE

HEY!

KRII KRII

FWIP

THOK
GAH!
CLOP CLOP
CLOP CLOP

R-RE-TREAT!
RE-TREAT!
ARE YOU SURE ?!
WE MANAGED TO INJURE GEUN-TAE! THAT'S PLENTY.
WE'LL RETURN ANOTHER TIME.
IT'S TOO DANGEROUS TO GO UP AGAINST *THAT.*

Whoa...
THEY'RE WITH-DRAW-ING...
THAT GUY'S NO ROOKIE...
I TOLD YOU, HE'S THE THUNDER BEA—
HAK!

HAK, YOU CAME!
TOK
SURE.

I WAS IN THE AREA, SO I DROPPED BY.
GLAD THE TIMING WORKED OUT.

HOW'S GEUN-TAE?
W...
WELL...

TO BE HONEST ...
...HIS INJURIES ARE QUITE SEVERE.
MURMUR...

HE TOOK THREE ARROWS IN THE BACK. HE'S LUCKY TO BE ALIVE.
HIS RECOVERY WILL BE DIFFICULT.
I...
...DON'T THINK GENERAL GEUN-TAE WILL BE ABLE TO FIGHT ANYMORE.
NO WAY!
SAY IT ISN'T SO, BOY!
IT'S MY FAULT...
LORD GEUN-TAE GOT HURT BECAUSE OF ME.
YUN...
PLEASE...

SAVE LORD GEUN-TAE!
SMASH

LADY YUNO!

NO, NO...

LORD GEUN-TAE...

WE'RE TOLD HE WAS WOUNDED IN KIN PROVINCE.

THEY SAY HE CAN'T BE MOVED.

IMPOSSIBLE!

NOT OUR LORD GEUN-TAE—!

GEUN-TAE IS BADLY INJURED?!

A MESSENGER BROUGHT THE NEWS THIS MORNING.

SOUTH KAI'S SOLDIERS WERE DRIVEN BACK, BUT THEN MADE A SURPRISE ATTACK ON THE GENERAL.

AND HIS CONDITION IS CRITICAL?
YES. IT'S UNLIKELY HE'LL BE ABLE TO GO INTO BATTLE ANYMORE.

THAT IDIOT ...

...

KING SU-WON ...
THE EARTH TRIBE TERRITORIES WILL BE AT THE FRONT LINES OF THIS WAR.
GENERAL GEUN-TAE HAS AN UNCANNY ABILITY TO DRAW PEOPLE TO HIS SIDE. IF HE'S TAKEN DOWN BEFORE THE WAR EVEN BEGINS...
...THE EARTH TRIBE WILL INSTANTLY COLLAPSE.

THIS IS WHEN WE NEED TO PREPARE OURSELVES AND UNIFY THE FIVE TRIBES.

BUT NOW, ON TOP OF KING SU-WON SHOWING SYMPTOMS, GENERAL GEUN-TAE HAS BEEN INJURED.

THIS IS AN IMMENSE BLOW.

YOUNG LADY.
ZENO ...

WHAT'S WRONG?
WHAT ARE THESE COFFINS?
SHA
SLIDE...

GIJA ?!
Ah!
SINHA ?!
JAEHA ?!
BUT WHY —?
THE END OF THEIR LIVES HAS COME.
THE END OF...
LOOK. THEY TOO...

SU-WON...
MEI-NYAN...
FOOM

FWOOSH
!
HIRYUU PALACE IS...
ZENO?!
WHERE ARE YOU?!
FOOSH

ALL OF YOU...
VOOM
JOLT
HUFF... HUFF...

Huff...

A DREAM ...

WHAT IS IT, YONA?

EEAAGH!!

ARE YOU ALL RIGHT, YOUR HIGHNESS?!

SWIPE

GUH!

SKRRK
DID HE DO ANYTHING INAPPROPRIATE?
HEY! GIJA!
NO, NOT AT ALL. I WAS JUST STARTLED.
HOW DARE YOU STARTLE HER HIGHNESS!
Gah!
LET GO! IS ALL THE FREE TIME GETTING TO YOU?!
...

THANK GOODNESS...
THEY'RE ALL OKAY...
YOUNG LADY?
DID YOU HAVE A SCARY DREAM?
ZENO, LISTEN...
YONA.
ADVISOR KEISHUK HAS COME.
WANT TO SEE HIM?

FORGIVE MY COMING SO LATE AT NIGHT.

WHAT IS IT?
I HAVE A REQUEST.
...
HIS MAJESTY'S HEALTH IS DECLINING.

BY ALL RIGHTS, HE SHOULD BE RESTING RIGHT NOW.
BUT HE'LL MOST LIKELY GO TO THE BATTLE-FIELD.
I CANNOT STOP HIM.
WHAT DO YOU WANT ME TO DO?

I'D LIKE YOU TO STAY BY HIS SIDE...

...DURING THE BATTLE IN SOUTH KAI.

KEISHUK, WHAT ARE YOU SAYING?

IF THE WORST OCCURS ...

...AND SOMETHING HAPPENS TO HIS MAJESTY ...
...I'D LIKE YOU TO COMMAND KOHKA'S ARMY.
CHAPTER 210 / THE END

BONUS CHAPTER: A SPRING PARTY

A GUEST CAME TO FUUGA TODAY.
HE'S LORD HAK'S FRIEND.
THIS IS LORD SU-WON. TRY NOT TO BE RUDE.

HE SAID TO TRY NOT TO BE RUDE.
HOW RUDE! WE'D NEVER BE RUDE.

WE'LL SHOW HIM THE BEST TIME!
WE SURE WILL!

AAAH!

WHAT THE HELL ARE YOU DOING?!
WE'RE SMOTHERING OUR GUEST IN FLUFFINESS!
GUEST
THIS IS THE WIND TRIBE'S GREATEST FORM OF HOSPI-TALITY!

BATTERED
THAT WAS QUITE FUN.
WAS IT, THOUGH?
SEE?

HE'S OF NOBLE BIRTH.

IS HE IMPORTANT?
YES.

DO IMPORTANT PEOPLE KNOW EVERYTHING?
THEY DO. SU-WON IS REALLY SMART.

DO YOU KNOW WHO LORD HAK IS IN LOVE WITH?
WE'RE DONE HERE!

THE WIND TRIBE'S GREATEST FORM OF HOSPITALITY IS OUR BATHS!
IT'S TIME FOR SOME NAKED BONDING!

DON'T WORRY, IT'LL ONLY BE US WITH YOU. WE'LL SHOW YOU THE BEST TIME.
SHUT

I THINK HE REJECTS HIS FIANCÉE, AYAME, BECAUSE SHE'S NOT THE PERSON HE'S IN LOVE WITH.
HAK HAS A FIANCÉE?

HE DOES, BUT THE WIND TRIBE GIRLS ARE ALL STILL OBSESSED WITH HIM. HE TRULY IS A HEARTBREAKER.

WHEN I ASKED HIM TO DESCRIBE HIS IDEAL GIRL, HE SAID SOMEONE WHO ISN'T A LOT OF TROUBLE. CAN YOU BELIEVE IT? HOW IS A 13-YEAR-OLD SO COOL?

THE WIND TRIBE'S GREATEST FORM OF HOSPITALITY IS OUR FOOD!
MUNCH
EAT UP.

WHAT'S THAT?
THEY'RE DRINKING A TASTY LIQUID FROM THAT POT THROUGH THOSE BAMBOO STRAWS.

I'D LIKE TO TRY IT.
I'M AFRAID IT'S FOR ADULTS. YOU'RE STILL TOO YOUNG, LORD SU-WON.
BUT SOMEONE MY AGE IS DRINKING IT.
Mmm...

ARE YOU AN ADULT, THEN?
DESPITE APPEARANCES, YES.
WHO'S HE?
NO IDEA...

A wandering old man who sneaks into parties for free food.

THE WIND TRIBE'S GREATEST FORM OF HOSPITALITY...
...IS OUR PILLOW FIGHTS!
THE PERSON WHO THROWS DOWN THE MOST WINS!

NORMAL PILLOWS ARE BORING, SO WE FILLED THEM WITH RICE.
GRANDPA WILL CLOBBER YOU FOR WASTING FOOD.
ANYONE WHO CAN STUFF THE THUNDER BEAST INSIDE ONE WILL RECEIVE A HAK HUG PILLOW!

GULP...

IT WAS A TRULY INTENSE SHOW OF HOSPITALITY.
I SEE.
MUNCH
WHOSE HUG PILLOW DID HAK WIND UP BEING?

BONUS CHAPTER / THE END

Hak, did you really become Su-won's hug pillow?
Tell me all about it.
BECKON

Afterword

HELLO! MY LIFE CONTINUES TO BE HECTIC. THANK YOU FOR ALL OF YOUR SUPPORT.
Kabu has been in a playful mood, and Pal has taken to hiding between people's legs.
SWIPE
IN AUGUST, I HAVE PLANS TO OPEN A *YONA* ART EXHIBITION IN OSAKA, BUT I WONDER IF IT'LL GO WELL...

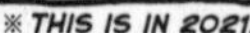
※ THIS IS IN 2021.

I'VE OPENED MINI ART EXHIBITIONS IN TOKYO AND FUKUOKA, BUT I HAVEN'T BEEN ABLE TO ATTEND ANY DUE TO CURRENT CIRCUMSTANCES AND SCHEDULING ISSUES.

Thank you so much to everyone who sent flowers to the exhibition sites!
Move aside, Kabu...
MUNCH

I REALLY WANTED TO GO TO THE TIE-IN CAFÉ WE DID DURING THE 2019 STAGE PRODUCTION.

Unfortunately, I couldn't make my schedule work out.

I'M SURE MANY OF YOU READERS CREATE THINGS OF YOUR OWN. HOW DO YOU FEEL WHEN YOU CREATE SOMETHING?

I START BY COMPLETELY FORGETTING HOW TO DRAW COMICS.

I FEEL LIKE I SIT ON THE BEACH FOR A LONG TIME WITHOUT STEPPING INTO THE OCEAN THAT IS *YONA OF THE DAWN*.

AM I... REALLY THE ONE WHO'S BEEN DRAWING YONA OF THE DAWN?

I'M UNABLE TO STAY FOCUSED.

Wanna play?

I get nervous, but I can't panic, because then I wouldn't be able to draw anything.

BY THE TIME I BRING BACK A STORY, UNSURE OF WHETHER IT'S GOOD OR BAD, SO MUCH TIME HAS PASSED IN THE REAL WORLD THAT I ONLY HAVE A DAY OR TWO TO CREATE THE MANGA PAGES. I FEEL LIKE TARO URASHIMA.

What? I have to turn it in tomorrow? Ha ha ha... By the way, what do you think of this?
Um... I think you should tweak how that's presented.
Sister

THEN, WHILE I'M DRAWING, I FORGET HOW TO SWIM ONCE AGAIN.

I'VE KIND OF LEARNED WHICH STORIES ARE GOOD AND BAD BASED ON YOUR REACTIONS. (ALTHOUGH A HUNDRED PEOPLE WILL HAVE A HUNDRED DIFFERENT OPINIONS.)

EACH TIME THIS HAPPENS, IT TAKES ME LONGER TO SWIM, SO FOCUSING IS MY BIGGEST HURDLE.

Don't abandon my storyboard.

Stay healthy.

Stay calm.

CREATING SOMETHING REQUIRES A STABLE MIND AND GOOD HEALTH.

I HOPE YOU'RE ALL TAKING CARE OF YOURSELVES.

Kabu steals my chair.

AFTERWORD / THE END

About the chapter 207 image that was originally in color... My assistants mistook him for Keishuk and some of my readers thought he was Hak. Sorry, it's actually Jaeha... I'd never draw a mysteriously long-haired Hak for a chapter page out of the blue. (LOL)

—Mizuho Kusanagi

Born on February 3 in Kumamoto Prefecture in Japan, Mizuho Kusanagi began her professional manga career with *Yoiko no Kokoroe* (The Rules of a Good Child) in 2003. Her other works include *NG Life*, which was serialized in *Hana to Yume* and *The Hana to Yume* magazines and published by Hakusensha in Japan. *Yona of the Dawn* was adapted into an anime in 2014.

YONA OF THE DAWN

VOL.36

Shojo Beat Edition

STORY AND ART BY
MIZUHO KUSANAGI

English Adaptation/Ysabet Reinhardt MacFarlane
Translation/JN Productions
Touch-Up Art & Lettering/Lys Blakeslee
Design/Philana Chen
Editor/Amy Yu

Printed in Canada

Published by VIZ Media, LLC
P.O. Box 77010
San Francisco, CA 94107

10 9 8 7 6 5 4 3 2 1
First printing, June 2022

ratings.viz.com RATED T TEEN

PARENTAL ADVISORY
YONA OF THE DAWN is rated T for Teen and is recommended for ages 13 and up. This volume contains violence and suggestive themes.

viz.com

shojobeat.com

A **Publisher's Weekly** bestseller!

What happens when the hottest boy in school *...is a girl?!?*

Find out in these 3-in-1 collections of the hit shojo series!

Hana-Kimi

Story & Art by HISAYA NAKAJO

Mizuki Ashiya has such a crush on a track star named Izumi Sano that she moves from the U.S. to Japan to enroll in the all-male high school he goes to! Pretending to be a boy, Mizuki becomes Sano's roommate...

...but how can she keep such a big secret when she's so close to the guy she wants?

IN STORES NOW!

3-in-1 Vol. 1 ISBN: 978-1-4215-4224-9
3-in-1 Vol. 2 ISBN: 978-1-4215-4225-6
3-in-1 Vol. 3 ISBN: 978-1-4215-4229-4